A RIVER ONCE MORE

A RIVER ONCE MORE

Poems By
Matthew Campbell Roberts

MoonPath Press

Copyright © 2019 Matthew Campbell Roberts

All rights reserved. No part of this publication may be reproduced, distributed, or transmitted in any form or by any means whatsoever without written permission from the publisher, except in the case of brief excerpts for critical reviews and articles. All inquiries should be addressed to MoonPath Press.

Poetry
ISBN 978-1-936657-46-9

Cover photo of the Methow River,
south of Mazama, WA,
by Matthew Campbell Roberts

Author photo by Gregory Macdonald
Book design by Tonya Namura using Gentium Basic

MoonPath Press is dedicated to publishing the finest poets living in the U.S. Pacific Northwest.

MoonPath Press
PO Box 445
Tillamook, OR 97141

MoonPathPress@gmail.com

http://MoonPathPress.com

For friends, family, and teachers who helped me along the way.

Table of Contents

I Return to the Feather River to Fish with My Father	3
Pistol River Estuary	4
Night Highway, Yakima River	5
Out of Emptiness	6
A River Once More	7
Thoughts	8
Back to Burley Creek	9
The Lost Valley	11
Zen Rock Garden: A Roethke Memorial	12
Dungeness Spit	13
Alt-Country: Bumping Lake to Wenas Valley, Hugo to Carver	14
Side Channel	15
Farm on Biava Ave.	16
Kerouac's Mountain	17
Fence Lines	18
Photograph of My Father: Chester, California, Circa 1976	20
One More for Napa	21
Chuckanut Creek	22
The Coast	23
Storm at Dash Point	24
Overlook	25
At Carver's Grave	26
A Branch for Winter	28
Beach Access	29
Burley Lagoon	30
Blue Hills like the Sea in August	31

In the Killdeer's Cry	32
Kennewick Man	33
Key Peninsula	34
Mayfly Dusk	35
The West Fork	36
After Reading a Poem by Robert Sund	37
North Fork of December	38
Light Pollution	39
Last Storm	41
Sidereal Days	42
Near Sprague	43
Sounds	44
The System	46
Larches	47
The Saltchuck	48
Vignettes from the North Cascades	49
Pickers	51
Conservation Labor on Early Winters Creek	52
The Great Bend, Tombstone Territory	54
Stillwater	55
Henry and John Thoreau on the Concord and Merrimack Rivers	57
Backwater	58
Lake Berryessa, California, Circa 1976	59
At Night, the Sea Takes on Another Light	61
The Big Hole	62
Coulee	63
Elegy for a Grandfather I Never Met	64
Marine Layer	65
The News	66

Canyon Creek, North Cascades	68
Home Waters	70
Acknowledgements	73
Notes	75
About the Author	77

A RIVER ONCE MORE

I Return to the Feather River to Fish with My Father

I tried to call above the river's octaves
to tell you I almost landed one,
but you were too far upstream
casting to an eddy behind a boulder,
no face, or recognizable body,
just the rod tip's little snaps
engaging in the possibility of trout.

You always said, "Fish the close water first,
then work your way out."
Such plain advice seems right
as I try to make sense of distance
and get the scene straight, so I can
see your face dancing in the current light,
but I can hardly remember.

You drove us over washboard roads,
the VW bus overheating on the pass,
as we passed all those peaks and streams.
I wanted to fill my life with them
and that sweet air from then on.
But your faceless figure by the boulder is gone,
now a rush of water against stone.

Father, what does it matter if I can't find
the road back to that river,
or other places you said we'd fish?
These endings are the same.
What you meant to say is
somewhere in the long waters,
in the high and far away.

Pistol River Estuary

Walking the beach, I found a sea lion
with a bullet hole in its head.
Its brown skin was like leather,
and eyes were tunnels where shore crabs emerged.
I panned the zenith for the shooter,
but only brown pelicans
traveled in undulating formations above the surf.
In the wind, I heard a song of desolation,
a song of souls in flight.
For the first time in my life I felt alone.
Death was a pulse of light.
Standing there, I grieved for a being
that had no choice.
I staged a driftwood lean-to around its body
and said, "live again."
The tide filled the estuary.
That solemn song arcing in my brain.

Night Highway, Yakima River

Last night I drove by the Yakima River
and rolled down the window to let out what was wrong.
Ice crept by; and where eddies formed,
a deep green penetrated to the bottom.
And even though it was near dark
I could see a farmhouse, on an oxbow,
like the place we rented on Biava Ave.
and should've bought
had my mother's parents loaned the money.

The smell of hay and bridle leather clung to mist;
not a sound in the fields,
only wind funneling down from dark canyons.
But who'd thought I'd be thinking
about that farm in California now?
Here off the highway in the dead of winter
and my father dying with cancer on Hood Canal.
Through the cold, I leaned into those years—
eyes closed with some of him—
those bottomless thoughts of what I should do.
Then the guilt stacks against me.

That house out there doesn't care.
I want to walk toward it,
knock on the door to see if anyone's home,
feel what it was like for my father to be well again,
and let things go for a while.
But there's no time. The cold is too cold,
and the missing sleep bares down.
And the road—
a forced life I told myself I'd never lead.

Out of Emptiness

I pulled off the road near the Skagit River,
below Newhalem,
and hiked through old growth
to a small waterfall at the mouth of a creek,
and sat there feeling empty
for no particular reason,
maybe a culmination of worries
about someone who said something that bothered me,
my destination that day, or the future.
I stretched out under the sky
listening to the river telling its story.
For those minutes, nothing mattered.
My mind became the river, then an island;
and at the edge of the current,
a blue heron stalking shallows for smolts.
We peered through the same glacial-green water
for a fish to dart by. After no luck,
he lifted his wings and lunged into the mossy corridor.
I held its orange eye in my eye
until he cleared the bend.
I was alone again looking skyward.
The sound of the waterfall
merged with the river's voices.
I glanced back at the island to where the heron
worked the shoreline,
and I realized that out of emptiness
something else could go on.

A River Once More

August. I was fishing the Chewuck River
thinking of an old friend
and how we sat around his fly tying bench,
drinking Scotch,
creating "working" flies, not pretty,
but they caught trout.
Our talk found Hemingway,
and with each glass we tried to sound more literary
recalling how Nick Adams
pierced a live grasshopper's thorax with a hook,
after tearing off its wings,
then spitting tobacco on it to screen his scent
before casting upstream.

I let my line snake slack
as my own hopper orbited the eddy on its side.
The current carried it near a boulder
when a golden cutthroat
erupted from the water and gulped it down.
Heat vapors danced
above rip-rap along the bank.
I felt the trout's head shaking down in the rocks
prying the hook loose.
Unnerved after losing that fish,
I crossed the river and headed for the road;
though, something else
followed me as I looked back
at my friend's cabin.
The wind rushed the cottonwoods,
and I stood there listening
to a new river singing,
and a life I once lived escaped into air.

Thoughts

He finds himself here each day
sitting by the bay watching the tide change.
Now, in old age, he doesn't feel rushed.
He listens to questions but doesn't need to answer.
He sits on a bench with the sea
reading water and commerce,
and breathing familiar smell of ebb tide.
But there are thoughts of how much time is left:
the unpaid bills on the kitchen table,
the unwritten will, and thoughts
of what might live on after he is gone.
What was here before and what remains?
What to change or leave the same?
Thoughts full of uncertainty dancing
quietly away in the wind
and returning as each day ends.
Soon there will be nothing,
and he will disappear into it
like a passing cloud
without anyone noticing.

Back to Burley Creek

I found the cabin door kicked open,
death inviting me inside.
My thoughts were nervous trout
darting for dark corners.
Cobwebs lifted like sails
as I scanned the dank kitchen—
a mural of powdery mold,
empty Black Label beer cans,
smashed plates,
and yellow newspapers—
to where a four-point buck,
knocked from the wall,
gazed through a stained ceiling.

An old man lived here once,
slouched in his blue-flannel shirt,
canvas fishing hat cocked sideways,
and black-framed glasses,
lenses thick as ice, pointing to a pool
he said I could fish.
Burley Creek was my refuge
from drunken words,
and lamps hurled through picture windows.
Here, time grew into itself
like blackberry vines
creeping beneath cedar shingles.
Here, steelhead tilled gravel
against dark currents.

Now decades later, I'm back
skinning leaves from an alder branch,
wrapping mono around its tip,
lobbing a nymph
into an undertow. The dizzy eddies

go round and round.
Everyone is gone.
Loss is a confluence of shadows
passing through me.
And waters that kept us,
sing about nothing.
And the far gray light,
strained by alders,
reaches for sunken stones.

The Lost Valley

On a day when morning clouds conceal distance,
you walk to a clearing after the river recedes
where debris marks high water.
Beneath the undercut bank, a stew of leaves
and sand erupt in turbulence
as cottonwood roots dangle in midair.
Dislodged stones clack along the bottom.
A pair of mergansers ferry to the far shore
and you remember how, before the flood,
a friend said goodbye
as she headed for the high country on her horse.
She was tired of "life's bullshit"
and wanted to find a lost valley and camp there.
All her years held those words.
A packer thought he saw her near Jack Mountain,
deep in the North Cascades.
Some night, maybe you'll sit by a fire,
looking up at stars through a canopy of trees,
and listen to water circling back on itself,
and dream of being lost
in a cold world with only darkness to follow.

Zen Rock Garden: A Roethke Memorial
Bloedel Reserve, Bainbridge Island, Washington

*One looks so long at an object...that you become the object
and it becomes you; it's an extension of consciousness.*
—Theodore Roethke

Rock sentinels rise from white sand
like coastal haystacks.
The raked lines around stones are clouds
uplifting gray granite peaks.
The pool's currents edge shoreward.
I listen to this dry sea sing
of shore pines burning in the wind.
There's no mark of tragedy, no reckoning,
only quietude. In this falling hour,
finches fly in and out of gourd birdhouses.
Death is not a lingering stranger here.
A red-flowering currant feels no guilt
as it leans toward the afterlight.
And the trumpeter swans see their reflections
on the glassy surface of the moon.
The Self flashes in the cottonwoods
and the weeping cyclamen
bows its head in shifting shade.
A song lifts from the pool's white granules
like rain feeding a bed of coals.
The body becomes smoke stirring over
buried stones. A varied thrush
whistles from a heaven of twigs and burls.
Who are you friend of the deep?
Can you help me find my way?
The incoming waves are calling now;
and before long, I realize how
it feels to reach into another life,
reach into the late hours
and let grief rise without regret.

Dungeness Spit

Light cannot shed the cold cadence
of receding surf.
Sandpipers peck tide-wash for worms.
Pebbles clatter from wave action.
I hear voices beyond the lighthouse
where the sea never dies. You can drift
this plane like a particulate strewn by wind.
The mind becomes a deep channel
carving its way back to how the world was once—
alive within the sanity of chaos.
Every day the marsh sips new tide
and shore crabs gather among pickleweed
to feed on green algae.
I sit on a log looking out at the Straight
waiting for something else to occur.

Alt-Country: Bumping Lake to Wenas Valley, Hugo to Carver

There's no hope of recovery in these foothills
or a last-gasp trout from Bumping Lake.
Below the dam, fish rise until an osprey's shadow
drives them down. The land is scarred
as mile-long thoughts fall from clear-cuts.
Sweat beads up, and you pull over at a culvert
where cutthroat hold in a no-name creek.

A dream claims a wind-bent cabin,
and you live there deciding the outcome is too morose.
The dream lingers on as you cut loose
dry-rotted beams, chink gaps between logs,
and fight off colonies of carpenter ants,
even threaten to kill their elusive queen,
but she's moved on to another shack.

Then what? The money goes dry, project
half-finished, and not a soul to cling to when
desperation sets in. You talk gibberish
to the same field day after day.
Once the dream fades, there's nothing left
but the motor ticking, so you drive
through Carver's Wenas hills that glow like white ash.

Headlights scan a moth's flight
up a dry creek bed
disappearing into hills that hide grief.
A meteor streams by
and the world's perfect stillness
hides dark corners of the universe.

Side Channel

In this silent corridor of stones
I found mountain lion tracks,
talons dredged deep in the dark sand,
at the edge of a small stream.
Beyond the half-light of the forest, a raven's knock
echoed through a sky of cottonwoods.
I followed the channel's history of flood and drought
by reading leaf fossils imprinted in shale,
unearthed from eroding banks.
I knelt and dipped my hand in the shallow water
and felt the glacier's icy pull.
There is life here where so few walk.
The tracks of deer and elk go on for miles.
When I came to where the stream merged
with the main stem of the river,
I sat on a rock as the sun warmed each stone
around me, and my hope renewed
that quiet places
carry us from one life to the next.

Farm on Biava Ave.

Through the night I dream of fields,
bulrush and ground fog,
where cattle sip from vernal ponds.
I climb a water tower
as barn swallows glide for mayflies
in green afterglow.
I carried their world of flight
to where years have gone,
sitting up late with fire,
waiting for the moon to guide me.

Kerouac's Mountain

Driving North Cascades Highway
I thought of Kerouac
wide awake at 2:00 a.m.
on Desolation Peak
as he paced
the fire lookout, corner to corner,
gazing through
his green reflection against dark cliffs
to pass time.
Guy wires hummed
violently in the wind.
Mist rising from forgotten creeks,
merged with space
he called "The Void"—
an awareness,
a loss of hope,
a world of shimmering terror
that followed
the rest of his life.

Fence Lines

I
Out at the twenty acres
digging post holes for my father,
ten bucks an hour,
rivers running through me.
Figuring my way out of this goddamn trailer,
back to the Peninsula,
to home that leads nowhere,
home you are afraid to call home,
home you return to flat on your ass,
the same one I left years back
telling everyone to get fucked.

II
Not a dream of anything comes in the night.
Estuaries boil with cutthroat
on flood tide.
A soaked dog groans in the rain.
Smoke swirls from a drum,
hands stained with bar oil,
shrieking owls,
creaking trees,
light another candle
stay awake late
to creosote on the wind.
O, but I wouldn't want any other life!
Friends fall in and out of mind.
How did I get so far out?

III
Day after day, same old Northwest song
rings from my saw,
take a break, sit on the tailgate,
chew beef jerky—

madronas shedding rusty skins,
huckleberries neck high,
split a truckload of wood,
make enough money for fuel and booze,
maybe another steelhead trip
up the Skagit.
Keep digging one hole at a time,
tighten that wire, son,
everything'll be fine.

Photograph of My Father:
Chester, California, Circa 1976

Near dark, and father and I are sitting at a picnic table
lined with a limit of rainbow trout.
The fish have lost their brilliance, eyes opaque,
and tails curled outward from lying in a creel.
Father fits the scene wearing a brown goose down coat
and hair not quite to his shoulders,
and his eyes seem to know mountains and rivers—
a world we disappeared into.

At the campground, rangers posted signs
warning people not to feed squirrels due to plague.
I remember a spring creek, with small snails
clinging to stone bottom, winding through a meadow.
And its sunlit currents, lazy and brackish,
with an acrid scent like creosote.
And the Feather River plunging
from pool to pool keeping me awake at night.

Those summer days say so much.
All my life I wanted my father to be someone else.
The years kept returning us to a lost world.
But he taught me how to fish
and love what can't be seen
like the sweet smell of rain before a flood,
or the sound of falling water
somewhere in the consuming darkness.

One More for Napa

I rise above oaks and waves of bleached grass
back to old days in Napa,
to plein air of vineyard and sky.
And the dark gulch
where Wild Horse Creek runs
over charred stones,
and wooden crosses staked by wrecked cars
that overshot turns.
On this road, riding in father's truck bed,
rolling from side to side,
as he drove too fast
squealing tires in and out of turns,
and mother tossing empties
from her window—
each beer can sailing, end over end,
to a graveyard below.
Rust breeding rust.
You think you can never go home,
then you drive this road
thirty years later and a familiar dream
notches space in summer wind.
Whose memory is right?
I'm thumping the cab's rear window,
"Slow down for god's sakes!"
Nobody listens as we weave up valley
chasing daylight
like some clown show—
no tears or apologies,
just another dream
where we all get out alive.

Chuckanut Creek

When you stand near this creek alone,
listen to the lisp of current.
What will your presence change?
Imagine your life again,
those who have come and gone,
their pale glances
spiraling toward some distant light.
At this time of night,
you can let go; this valley's waited
to show you far off ridges
where you could spend a life
standing at the rim of thought,
where nighthawks carve the evening.

The Coast

Boats that pulled last hauls decades ago
are marooned in meadows
and muck just out of tide's reach.
Dead standing cedars, bleached silver,
house the northern Saw-whet owl.
A cranberry bog sulks in unattended silence,
but its surface ripples
as a midge struggles to free its casing.
Nothing else moves.
Shore pines are bent and thinned
from scouring sea winds
and the last light bathes the shimmering stones.
Now the world begins
its procession over,
of deciding what will stay or go,
or what will form another life
for another time.
The self peels into wind and waves
as the slow journey unfolds
and some other wild,
splintering place emerges.
There are eternities in this vaporous sky—
too much gray for a land to absorb.

Storm at Dash Point

I watched a tanker cross the channel
between Vashon Island and Dash Point
as a pier fisherman, listening to a congested radio,
leaned into the wind and swells
that carried the Brant and Bonaparte's gulls to shore.
How easy a day like this can bring you back
to the self you once believed in.
Just to sit on a log and guess at the tide
or scavenge for sea glass and agates
at the edge of breakers. Or do nothing at all
and not worry about the news or work.
How easy it all goes by if you accept
the life that says, "This is who I am now."
And let the rest of the world
follow one storm after another.

Overlook

She pulled off the pass here one day,
a trace of spruce in the air,
and below, headwaters of a river.
The spring sun felt warm on her face
and rivulets made a trickling sound beneath snow.
She traveled a long way from home
not knowing where life would eventually take her.
Sitting there on the hood of her car,
she thought about her mother
and wished she could've seen these mountains.
Down in the valley there were pulses
of wind and intervals of unfamiliar silence.
And deeper, where the river
churned white through the gorge,
light played on tips of fir trees.
She leaned back against the windshield,
gazed into blue space,
feeling how this place was part of her now.
She wanted to remember
this first time, when her life became her own,
gathering and releasing
each breath of impenetrable sky.

At Carver's Grave

It's all here, the Strait, the feel of country
worked in, and rough crusaders
whose headstones are lost to deep woods.
Riggers, whistle punks, and gyppo loggers—
they knew the ride was short but not free.
And the islands are here too with slopes and passages,
a few boats trolling for blackmouth
off the shelf—this is how life should be.

Who cares if there are whitecaps
or fog in the Straight—you go anyway.
It could be this easy:
pick any island, get a job to pay bills,
rent one of those salt-bleached cabins,
paint a mailbox like a fish,
know the postman by name,
and not worry about retirement or anything else.

Maybe fix up an old wood boat,
nothing fancy, just a runabout
with room for mooching gear,
a cooler of beer, and a canopy
in case you get caught in a gale.
That happens, you know.
You hear about how it was a mill pond
then all of a sudden a squall kicks up.

Or just the other day, those two guys
who went down in a skiff,
checking crab pots, the paper said.
Wind came out of nowhere.
They weren't from around here, I guess.

Some bodies are never found,
and the ones that are,
look like no one anybody knew.

A Branch for Winter

A branch you never noticed before,
even though you've walked
this trail your whole life,
hangs over the river
bearing heaviness of snow,
dipping once in awhile
to feel the current's pull.
Remember times when
people seemed close,
when mornings made the world
indifferent to what you
thought mattered.
Now voices follow your thoughts
through a mesh of hanging moss,
and will not leave.
This is how a friend should be
on a day that asks,
"Who will remember you?"

Beach Access

The pickleweed and stickleback spines
were lost long ago to shore wash.
The patch-job cabin on pilings, where an old woman
lived among peonies and wild rosehips,
stored jars of pickled eggs and pigs' hoofs in the hall.
A dozen cats were perched on sills,
heads locked between window bars
as stained curtains caught gusts of heat.
The sills set a sort of stage
for cats, and their black and brown masks
danced to the invisible vapors.
They watched me without a blink
drag my skiff down the beach
away from the old woman's toxic breath
and the soft purple bags under her eyes
that held a lifetime of grief.
The theater of longings
mingling with her absence of words.

Burley Lagoon

Near the mouth of Burley Creek, where Francis lived,
a spear carved from an alder branch
kills flounder in the tide flats.
A skull from a herring gull means you've arrived.
These are the sloughs of my youth,
ripe with salmon carcasses, sculpins,
backyard tire fires, and willows.

I watched him sitting on a fir stump
beneath a moss-saddled roof
that beetle-infested beams and posts
strained to hold up. He was lighting a fire
to evade the benthic darkness,
illuminating writhing blackberry vines
as mice gnawed at the cabin's rafters.

We trespassed fields and hopped fence lines,
eluding old man Williams's
shotgun blasts of rock salt,
to reach the estuary
where oyster farmers raked creosote shores
in lee of night—
apparitions rising from mud.

Maybe I'm wrong about all this,
but there was no way out for you.
If I could've helped, I didn't;
the lagoon cast its spell long ago.
The cold moon carries corpses to the other side,
and we dream of endless returns
where we don't suffer alone.

Blue Hills like the Sea in August

Tonight we remember
our postapocalyptic dreams.
We flare above unthinkable
blue hills and nictate
moth-like over haystacks
returning to sea,
asking for life again,
the same love we said we'd not lose
to the chromic beaches
we seine for hope.
And sometimes it's there,
in a Galapagos of space,
as you appear to tell me
how to recover from
disconsolate miles
teaching us how to leave
whatever has kept us.

In the Killdeer's Cry

The valley's meadows braid your memory
like summer point bars.
It happens sometimes, people move
here never to leave; their faces rescued
from a forgotten range.
Your way was harder, being lost
far off in the hills alone,
with no stars, only a pictograph leaning
from its rock shelf
calling you farther from home.
When it's time, there's a choice, we say.
We hold words
so long they forget their meaning
in shadow waters
where caddis flies oscillate at dusk.
Is it right to say there is an edge
our lives pass over
where time evades darkness
and all hurt ceases?
Is it right to say we missed you, brother?
You are not alone now.
In the killdeer's cry you glide
over silver currents.

Kennewick Man

Here we go again, Kennewick Man,
the paper says you are free now.
It says you traveled through an ice age,
over scree fields before the Columbia
dredged your clay tomb.
You crossed bridges of time to an old world
with a calcified arrow in your hip.
Even after the ice dams collapsed,
and the Lake Missoula flood
carved desert basins,
before concrete and barges
raised Grand Coulee Dam,
your story lodged in Precambrian sediments.
If you could speak
with your shattered jaw,
you could let the world know
there's no way back:
the ice sheets melted,
glaciers receded into caves,
and the land bridge
submerged beneath the sea.
Let them know I heard your last cry,
as you traveled rivers
wider than the Nile and Euphrates,
finding your way back
to some lost plain
where all endings and beginnings start.

Key Peninsula

We played out our fathers' roles as shipwrights
and brush pickers who spent paychecks at last call.
We poached dark kings and chum from Minter Creek,
"smokers," we called them, left to rot on our porches.
We've tried to move on from those days
by scraping barnacles from our stolen skiffs
and skimming spruce oars over lost estuaries,
passing shacks on pilings where holdouts lived
on cheap whiskey and desperation.
We trolled plugs deep off Devil's Head for blackmouth,
and held the night in our hands.
Let these corroded oar locks
groan up at the moon leaving our bodies behind.
Row this breeze with me now, old salt,
through dark hours that carry our song,
and we'll bury this hatchet
deep beneath a bed of sand dollars.

Mayfly Dusk

In the mayfly dusk,
I hiked up river
as far as light would allow
catching redband rainbows.
Their orange fins
and purple parr marks
painted the canyon
pocket water.

The West Fork

Far off, another life calls
when moon finds its way back
to where you once lived.

Nobody knows the path you've chosen.
Maybe someone once said,
"You should've done it this way."

Here, you follow endless trails
through scree fields and mountains—
one drainage leading to another.

There are creeks with no names
and generations of trout
never to see a human face.

Dead-standing firs
open wind's door and reach
for light beyond ridges.

Look into clear currents,
the silent stones,
this world calling you home.

Truth is where you stand.
Hold onto this place, friend,
you'll need it again someday.

After Reading a Poem by Robert Sund

On a fall morning,
I dreamt I saw him in a shack
boiling water for tea
and reading Zen poems
as maple leaves twirled in the wind,
descending to Disappearing Lake.

I roamed inside his hut
and tapped walls as restless mice
rustled in their bays.
I felt ashamed that I was there—
a stranger waiting for a ghost
to return to an abandoned home.

Walking high grass to tideline,
where all silences live,
I tried to recall what I wanted to ask him,
but what was it?
I sat there for hours with the sun
reaching beyond fields.

When tide crept up the bank,
I launched a skiff, pushing off with an oar,
not sure where I was going.
The eel grass waved me through
a maze of channels—
and a life of words on the breeze.

North Fork of December
For Tom and Matt Frazier, fly fishing the Nooksack River

He kneeled among rocks by the North Fork,
holding a Dolly Varden just below the surface—
the orange marabou fly waving in its mouth.
Through a cold reflection,
he examined the fish to feel its white-tipped fins
fanning glacial current.
I remember him looking back at me,
in the white spray, as he let the char loose.
I didn't know that day would be our last together.
He drowned beneath a Montana sky
so shallow the earth almost forgot his name.
Some days, when I return to fish the upper reaches,
and window-clear water
slides over boulders stable as time,
I hear them in the trees,
where wind and other voices live,
as the forest turns morning's light into shafts.

Light Pollution

We were college freshmen,
the three of us laughing,
swigging beer, driving dusty back roads
through a picket of lightless pines
with oldies cranking on the Fairlane's
radio outside of Cheney.

We had Billy's astronomy professor's telescope,
the one not supposed to leave campus
and worth more than our cars.
He borrowed it for his star chart project,
a half dome looking thing
like the head of R2-D2.

I rode in the backseat with my arm around R2
holding it tight through the washboard
as we bopped and twisted,
did the mashed potato, spilling beer
on my crotch like it was our last
dance at the grange sock hop.

I'm not sure what we thought we'd see that night.
The yellow glow from the dash
flickered with each pothole,
and one of our headlights peered off into tree tops,
the other disappearing into a zenith
dissolved by interstellar dust.

When we finally arrived at a clearing,
or the car stalled, I don't remember,
a place Jason said his dog was mauled
by a pack of coyotes, we mounted R2's head
to the hood and pointed her one good eyeball
up at the waning gibbous moon.

What we saw were craters
and mountains, like we were really there
making our own lunar landing.
We found Cassiopeia, Orion's Belt,
and what we thought were the moons of Jupiter,
turned out to be splotches of dried beer on the lens.

For the first time, we believed in ourselves—
we were invincible beyond doubt.

Last Storm

There is a farm on the Palouse where no one lives.
Wind blows storms of dust
over hills as the cracked earth asks, "How can a silo
outlive a family more than once?"
When drought came, it made every day
follow thoughts of rain.
Tumbleweeds piled against a barn door—
to a bent crease of light
revealing an old International
that once raked its rusted tines across potato fields.
Father wanted to stay;
he knew each losing acre by wrinkled touch.
Its dark soil scattered downwind
like a thermal carrying mother's ashes.
We prayed for prisms
of irrigation spray to become a thunderhead.
That was our last storm together.
Others would follow,
whispering, "Remember those rumbling years?"

Sidereal Days

Because we are not dead,
we push our carts toward progress,
janitors of the subterranean,
sweeping earth from earth.
We drink tea in the courtyard
beneath eucalyptus trees,
feed the noble Koi their dish of sky.
Windbreak towns, where some of us
were born among windmills and rust,
dangle in our minds
like crop names from a fence.
Every day we follow these fields
into bottomless swales
where barn swallows
feed from the air we breathe.

Near Sprague

Walking through the night,
I pass a grain elevator where shadows
talk and sweep and kill the clock.
The night is day inside.
The land always needing more
than they can give.
They wait for a container,
"last load," calls the foreman,
as smoke hauls their heaviness to the coast.
Roads are worn to stones
and ditches are alive with star thistle.
They hear the uplift of a dead sea swell,
and look out frameless windows
to a wrecked schooner.
Soon, the old crew will
rebuild a town to cheers and sighs,
and the marching band
will lift hometown spirits
carrying their fight into starved hills.

Sounds

Alone at the cabin on Hood Canal,
I heard screaming from the backwoods,
a cougar, nothing to worry about;
although, the more I listened,
it sounded like "Help, Help!"
I thought of an old paperback
on cryptozoology, *Bigfoot Among Us,*
or something like that.
In it were testimonials by people
who had run-ins with Sasquatch.
One guy near Mount St. Helens,
said boulders were hurled at his truck.
Another hiker mentioned a beast
with red eyes peering
through the vestibule of his tent.
As I lay there, in and out of dream,
without a drop of alcohol to stave off nerves,
I thought about driving home one night,
on a dark peninsula road
and I'd hit bigfoot—*isn't this in a movie?*
But when I imagined it,
the beast didn't total the car
because I was driving slow in the rain,
the night, the curves,
even though I'd been drinking.
Then I stood looking down at the thing.
No blood. No cars went by.
Only the miserable rain shooting down
like sparks in front of the headlights.

I jumped back in the car and thought about
reporting it to the police,
but I imagined newspapers hounding me,
the phone ringing off the hook,

or maybe they'd smell booze.
I saw a headline, "Drunk Man Kills Skunk Ape."
Even my family thought I'd lost it.
I decided against turning myself in
and tried to forget the sounds
or the "Help" part anyway.
I closed the window and went back to bed
and forgave myself for doing nothing
but sitting in the sober darkness
frightened by the other end of night.

The System

We heard about a mime who took his life here
as people pointed and laughed.
We passed pools of standing water,
where rushes grew at their edges.
Cirrus clouds whisked into a maze
over ploughed land beyond.
It wasn't what we thought,
no dirt floor juke joints,
or card rooms begging for air,
but it wasn't bad either.
We didn't labor to acclimate,
or walk far to find space.
The day never quit on us.
Nobody told us what to do.
We drank with cupped hands.
We didn't need to listen anymore
as we walked past ourselves
toward a latitude of festive lights.

Larches

Walking out of your life,
you hold words close
afraid of resurrecting bad years.
There's nothing left
in old places except light
where silence dwells.

I was thinking about living
like larches high up in the mountains,
on a sloped meadow
where nobody goes. How quiet the days
must be in dead of winter
when snow falls lightly on their boughs.

I would listen to wind
and its undulating syllables.
At night, voices of God
chant warnings of the future:
"Dig roots deeper."
And stars beam down signals.

This is how it is belonging to a place
and never leaving.
The world holds wasted years,
but you have to step
back from who you were
and reach for what's calling.

The Saltchuck

The slow mist unfolds reshaping
the known world.
I find old men from my youth
in worn oil-skin coats
skinning flounder and spitting tobacco.
They speak of ling cod
reeled from deep-fathomed caves,
of knucklebusters,
and the world's ancient currents,
of the saltchuck,
and slough sedge bending in rain,
of driftwood duck blinds,
and green-winged teal
planing in during winter storms.
I walk through their lives,
as the mist radiates with longing.

Vignettes from the North Cascades

I
Driving North Cascades Highway home,
late October,
end of another guiding season
on the Methow River.
Up the pass, snow sways
to some half-beat twang,
windows down,
one last look at Silver Star
climbing all that way alone,
knowing night will restore solitude—
the everness of wilderness.

II
A Chinook leaps from a roadside pool
clearing the earth below Newhalem,
"the deep green," fisherman call it,
leaves unfolding in the underwash.
How to get back?
No answer.

III
Driving rain.
Logging rigs mash orange
maple leaves on Highway 20.
Hard fields, hard sense,
find me here
this time broke, living in my truck—
things the currents take
and carry away.

IV
Pull off at the Cascade River bridge,
look down into
windows revealing char
still as stones,
a dark king, a buck
fights off two jacks
planing from bank to bank
then returning to guard
a female digging a redd.

A fisherman
slings his rig
of hot pink and orange
corky and yarn
upstream,
looks back, shakes his head
says, "They're all here,
but the party hasn't started yet."

V
Marblemount.
This is where locals slip from dark woods
cold as freestone streams,
bold as haphazard moraines,
and what about the off-key clarinet?
The wet grass sips ground fog
gathering ceremonially in a field.
I walk a dirt road
listening for what might happen next.

Pickers

When it rains in Omak, gyp pickers sleep under blue tarps on cardboard beds scattered along the muddy edges of the Okanogan River. They've created a camp there hacking down pines and cottonwoods with axes and handsaws, left Budweiser empties in the weeds, and a crew passed out in the brush. On the muddy bank, a lone fishing rod rests its spine on forked branches as monofilament wavers in the current.

In an eddy behind a submerged log
where nobody notices,
a smallmouth bass strikes a blue damselfly.
There's nothing he's not seen:
the horse carcass hung up in a logjam,
the wino's promised last bottle,
and broken lawn chairs
left by fishermen too drunk to swim.

Conservation Labor on Early Winters Creek

I
Riparian restoration
working from knees
dredging holes
planting snowberry
and Oregon grape
hold upright
pack dirt
untangle
red-osier dogwood
roots
soaking at creek's edge.

II
High noon, and we lean shovels
against a fence rail
and sit in shade of pines.
I dip my hand and drink creek water,
splashing it on my face.
A golden stonefly
dries its wings on a boulder;
far upstream, a small trout rises
for a bee but misses.
The crew boss throws me a roll
of yellow caution tape:
"Come Memorial Day,
these plants will be trampled!"

III
Mountains are lost in their godliness
against Methow sky.
Nothing but granite and dust
and alpine firs that somehow live in crags.
Some places we hold so deep

that time and meaning become lost.
But eventually, thoughts
find us again, waking or working,
should we return to those
spaces when nothing else remains,
where all that's left
is memory's uncertainty,
or streams of clouds on their way.

The Great Bend, Tombstone Territory

Looking across the bend
at the Skokomish River mouth,
root wads are washed clean
and steelhead out-migrate
seeking salvation
feeding on shadow clouds of sand lance
filling bays like lanyards of rain.

In the music of seeps and shale,
fossilized cutthroat bones sing our fate.
Look out at the wildness of place—
a gull's taunt, surf scoters diving for mollusks,
and ask what they know.
Let the reply of waves begin,
let the sibilance of streams
find restoration,
and accept what we've become.

Stillwater

My father holds on in deep sleep,
fighting for his life. In one limp hand,
a photo of a washed-out farm
near Bowie, Texas, where he stayed as a boy.
Our minds traveled through deep places
like the ranch for sale near Republic:
"Enough land we could all live on," he'd say.

He liked Curlew Lake country.
We went fishing there in August
and rented a cabin on a point.
The lake was shallow with coils
of milfoil providing cover
for largemouth bass snapping
blue damselflies copulating in flight.

There was a black and white cat
that sprang from the grass
and ambushed swallows
returning to their nests beneath the eves.
We sat there for hours looking at water,
sipping drinks, as boats trolled by
and bass cruised weedbeds.

Out of nowhere, a warm wind
picked up and rushed the pines
and the lake became its own again.
The docks creaked and clanked.
The coots held tight to the bank.
And I remember my father saying,
"This is where you can forget about it all."

When we left the lake,
my father drove gravel roads pulling off

at For Sale By Owner signs.
We walked each parcel like we owned them.
Sometimes he'd forget about a ranch,
settle for a cabin near the water,
and made plans right then and there.

Traveling home that night,
through dark mountain passes,
we talked about work and unfinished projects,
eventually settling
on the lake property he liked.
Somehow, in the dark alpine air,
something told me he wouldn't get that chance.

I held the photo of the farm where he lived,
looked at my father's chest
rising and falling with each shallow breath
as he lived those final hours
in a slow world of dream,
and I knew there was nothing left to say.

Henry and John Thoreau on the Concord and Merrimack Rivers

> *Gradually the village murmur subsided, and we seemed to be embarked on the placid currents of our dreams, floating from past to future as silently as one awakes to fresh morning or evening thoughts.*
> —Henry David Thoreau

John and Henry rowed downstream
of a waning century
symbolized by an old man
wearing a weathered brown coat,
fishing from a bank in falling light.
He was last generation
building log-hewed cabins on stilts
to stave off floods,
and he caught pickerel with a cane pole
beneath tangled willows.
How is it that nobody remembered him?
He was an inhabitant of a lost time,
disappearing without a sound.
The brothers sailed through his life,
through flooded meadows
of white water lilies,
and their own faces reflected
in tree-lined shadows like ghosts
against summer hills,
lessening with each sweep of the oars.
And there were moments
of timelessness, islands of ancient solitude,
days that never departed,
light wind lifting sails,
a journey of lasting silence.

Backwater

I walked from the mouth of Mission Creek
to a tailout below a stacked pool.
Three farm kids were chucking rocks
into riffles where chum salmon jostled
back and forth, loosening gravel.
The big kid bawls out, "Five bucks says you can't
drag one out ass backwards."
The skinny kid sheds his socks and sneakers,
wades up to his zipper,
reaches shoulder deep into the leaf-choked
swirl until his arm danced electric.
Both arms now are clamped above the salmon's tail,
"Hang onto him, man!"
a skittish boy calls from the bank,
but my money's not on the fish.
That boy is stronger than he looks,
all cord and bone,
living inside the struggle of give and take.
He's got the fish whipped now,
heaving the gasping carcass from the water.
Bent and wasted, it slaps the mud bank,
bucks a couple times until its gills—
choked with sand—begin to bleed.
And all eyes of the group stare,
"What are you gonna do with him now?"
the big one says, spearing the fish's eye with a stick.
"You owe me five bucks you bastard!"
"The hell I do,"
kicking the carcass into the creek
where it drifts snout first,
belly up, downstream, until its tail clips a sweeper,
spins from branch to branch,
before disappearing beneath a logjam.

Lake Berryessa, California, Circa 1976

We were trolling the shoreline
where oaks and chaparral
choked hillsides. My father,
and his hippie friend, Buddy,
smoked joints and slammed animal beers
to Fleetwood Mac rattling
from a portable cassette player.

I noticed Buddy's gang troll
dragging a clump of milfoil behind the boat.
He stood up to piss,
rocking the boat sideways,
and the motor's prop dug into mud
kicking up a mushroom cloud
ending any aspirations of catching fish.

We reeled frantically but still
snagged bottom as Buddy
hauled in a bird's nest of line, weeds, and lures.
"Sorry, dudes," he said, as laughter,
beers, and reefer ensued.
By now, batteries were low on juice,
and Stevie Nicks's voice played in slow-mo.

But I stayed tuned to the belief
that I could catch a trout
and lowered my bait down
columns of light
where my minnow twitched
back and forth trying to shed the hook
looped through its back.

I kept a lock on my rod
when I felt something tap my line.
Something big. And suddenly,

the pole lunged over the gunnel.
My father cut the throttle
and yelled, "Don't horse him in,
let him run if he wants to."

The trout peeled line from my reel,
turned, and orbited the boat.
I leaned back with pressure
fearing I might lose him.
In those intervals of time,
of give and take, I thought if I landed
the fish it would save my father's ass
and justify the fact that my mother would
believe that we were fishing
and not getting trashed.

When we arrived home in the dark,
my mother stood over the kitchen sink
in silence, doing dishes,
letting my father know she didn't
approve of his altered state.
But we had an ace up our sleeves,
a get out of jail free card,
a five-pound rainbow wrapped in newspaper.

I pulled the fish from its tomb
and held its stiff form above my head,
"Look what I caught!"
My mother sighed, and I could see
the corners of her mouth relax
as she held the Polaroid to record my catch.

I thought we were off the hook, but
she pulled a knife from the drawer,
pointed it at father,
"Clean the goddamn thing outside."

At Night, the Sea Takes on Another Light

Once more, walking at nightfall,
I'm lost in a mind of too many years.
What I thought to become
washed back on itself decades ago.
The sea batters the same dream
that sails for some other self
while I'm left here
punished for bad decisions.
Does it matter I'm not who I was?
Smoke from pulp stacks
says nothing changes.
I've been here too long
waiting for another night to arrive.
A gray face rises from clay.
Someone calls from
deep woods—
faces are streaks of green light.

The Big Hole

Thoughts take me back to the Big Hole River,
early twenties, road tripping
with barely money for beer and fuel,
and how I rode out an electrical storm
under cottonwoods in jean shorts,
clutching a fly rod and cursing
my friend who drove to Deer Lodge
to visit his brother in prison.

It's this way sometimes; you see parts of yourself
disappear with each storm,
like the valley you said you'd return to someday,
make a life, and never look back.
"Go on," a voice calls.
Nobody's there, of course,
no open sky, or sleeping in truck beds,
or a tavern in Dillon
where I danced with a woman
in a dusty parking lot to a shitty country band.

Even where stars guide moths to lost prairies,
never seen again, you believed
how there was always time.
Say you'll love this place
and take your chances,
then row into night's desert
looking for a way to resurrect a new life.

Coulee

In gray stillness a man stands at the edge
of a corral and sets a pail down.
As if out of habit,
he pumps orange water from a well,
though he sold his horses decades ago.
Now the night highway
hums and the vagrant thistle breathes
desperate desert air.
The man gazes up at the blurry
Milky Way and calls for Blue, an old ranch dog,
nowhere to be found.
On certain nights, winds from the Pacific
travel up the Columbia
and he remembers days at sea
on his grandfather's Constellation,
an old Chris-Craft
that smelled of teak and varnish.
And how they shot his
Winchester into stars from the stern.
Tomorrow he will wake early
and survey his 100 acres,
mend fence lines, and envision cattle
drinking from dry coulees.
And the spent tassels of grass
pray rain will bring back
something perennial to his lost river bed.

Elegy for a Grandfather I Never Met

Last night I traveled a ghost highway
to Bowie, Texas, to find my grandfather.
He was an electrician by trade,
but my father rarely talked about him
except to say he hated it when he sang
in the shower early mornings.

It was summer, and fireflies
zig-zagged beneath willow branches.
I walked by armadillo carcasses in ditches,
midnight chants of holy loneliness,
and a red moon rising from sand
to the cemetery on Campbell Street.

I sat on a concrete bench
with stillness, stars, and stones.
"Where are you?" I called.
"Why are you here?" a shape asked,
as it rustled beyond lamplight.
"What do you want to know?"

I felt something from the invisible,
a semblance of a man
from a black and white photo,
drinking martinis, with a bottle on the way,
after running wire all day
from one desolate place to another.

I held dried grass and soil in my hand
and watched the moon fall.
All the years and lost years
gathered and dissipated
beyond this plot of the unknown.

Marine Layer

Sailboats gunkhole shallow coves
around McMicken Island,
and shore crabs, trapped in tide pools,
scamper for shadows.
Sunlight breaks across the bow
as we cross Case Inlet
beyond our fathers who left the hard way.
We hear their voices
in the shifting wind, their words
in a rising tide.
We sing summer back to sand lance
and searun cutthroat
to the trail of alder smoke
stinging from last night's
beach fire. We sing for the shack
where a recluse
fought progress, and ancient firs
dangle roots
from eroding clay cliffs.
Somehow, time
is stilled here, and summer
offers its blessing,
as we peel line from our reels
and troll shorelines
for an underwater pulse—
the difference
between life and death.

The News

You never know how news will change your life.
Looking out at the Gulf Islands,
a storm that kept you awake at night racks windows.
You rise and imagine a beach cabin
on Saltspring Island, or Gabriola,
where you can write in peace,
and the ferry's foghorn is the only disruption.
But in the harbor, a sailboat rips at its buoy
like a dogfish trying to shake a hook.
You try to cut the shark loose,
so you can return to bed,
before it beats hell out the boat.
You see, these days are never long enough.
There's time to agree with your life,
time to see things for what they are,
not what they might've been.
The world has seized up and nobody cares;
everybody's consumed with their own worries.
You can say, fuck it, but that's too easy.
And then you turn on the radio,
as Charlie Haden's bass fades,
and the news cuts in reporting another human foot
washed ashore on a remote Canadian beach.
Nobody knows the count,
but they estimate 14 in the last decade.
Jazz returns, this time Brubeck's "Take Five"
but the storm doesn't care either way.
You'll sit here all morning and wait for a lull,
until a friend calls to meet for coffee,
but you won't mention the news
or the dogfish circling your mind.
Today, you'll forget everything you heard,
and the quiet islands,
and march through the rain,

as if nothing else matters, holding
the gray ceiling
on your shoulders—
driving forth with all your might.

Canyon Creek, North Cascades

I fished near Beebe's cabin,
old Forest Service guard station
near Canyon Creek
where Gary Snyder stayed years ago.
Wading miles upstream,
I skated a caddis across a deep pool
where a rainbow trout
ascended from green stones,
checked my fly, and vanished.

Time dimmed and I felt the forest's
glowing eyes
from old-growth branches.
And there were other hauntings,
cries and laughter,
ghosts of pickaxe dreamers
who marched along granite cliffs,
slashing devil's club,
carving scree trails to mining claims.

I wanted to keep casting
but a dark wall forced me back.
The current was strong,
and I lost footing
smashing my knee on a rock,
but adrenaline kicked in
as I staggered for the bank.

Once panic subsided,
my retinas widened to moonlight,
and I heard a distant car throttling
up the pass, and who I was
drifted toward some other stillness,

lost in the obscurity of night,
and the part that remained
merged with water.

Home Waters

You walk over green stones
into a new life.
Cottonwood leaves carry the year's
message downstream.
The dipper dives shallow currents for larvae.
There's no time for looking back,
the river says, move seaward
toward unconquerable light.

In a side channel, your own beginning
and detritus swirl
as you wade beaver's pool
and admire its fortress of
gnawed alder branches.
Let the island's forest
bathe you in its holy air.
Isn't this why we are here?

Now you cross the river for home
and walk the familiar
path until swallows turn invisible,
and the land you know
doesn't exist anymore.
Deer graze alfalfa fields;
white eyes glow in green dusk.
Anything is possible.

Acknowledgements

The author would like to thank Natalie Fedak, who helped with the overall layout of the manuscript, as well as many other editors of the following literary journals where some of the poems were previously published:

Clackamus Review: "Kennewick Man"

Clover: A Literary Rag: "One More for Napa," "Henry and John Thoreau on the Concord and Merrimack Rivers," and "Photograph of My Father, Chester, California, Circa 1976"

Cirque Journal: "A River Once More," "After Reading a Poem by Robert Sund," "Back to Burley Creek," "Kerouac's Mountain," "Out of Emptiness," "Storm at Dash Point," "The Coast," "The Lost Valley," "The West Fork," "The Big Hole," and "Zen Rock Garden: A Roethke Memorial"

Gathering of Voices Anthology: "North Fork of December"

Jeopardy: "Light Pollution"

The Methow Naturalist: "In the Kildeer's Cry"

StringTown: "Night Highway, Yakima River" and "At Carver's Grave"

Whatcom Places II Anthology: "A Branch for Winter" and "Chuckanut Creek"

Windfall: "Pickers"

Notes

The epigraph at the beginning of "Henry and John Thoreau on the Concord and Merrimack Rivers" (p. 57) was quoted from Thoreau in his book, *A Week on the Concord and Merrimack Rivers.* This poem is a homage to the brothers' voyage and lives.

In "Zen Rock Garden: A Roethke Memorial" (p. 12) the epigraph was quoted from *In a Dark Time: A Film About Theordore Roethke.* It was directed by David Myers for McGraw-Hill Films. The poem itself figuratively describes the Japanese garden (or referred to as a Zen rock garden in the poem) located at the Bloedel Reserve on Bainbridge Island. The location of the Japanese rock garden was once a swimming pool where Roethke died August 1, 1963.

About the Author

Matthew Campbell Roberts was born and reared in Napa, California, and attended a one-room schoolhouse set in the middle of a vineyard.

Later, after working as a carpenter and fly-fishing guide, he attended Western Washington University and Eastern Washington University where he received a Master of Fine Arts Degree. He currently teaches college composition and creative writing courses.

His poems and other works appear in various literary journals and anthologies. Roberts has spent decades fly fishing on Puget Sound and Northwest rivers, and many of his poems reflect those days and memories. Since we live in a time of environmental disruption, his work stands as witness to the various gradients of degradation.

There are also poems in this book about the memory of his father and their experiences together. Although many of these poems are somewhat regional, their themes of lost time, grief, and self-renewal, are universal. This book is about returning to the river in mind and spirit.

The author lives in Bellingham, Washington.

www.ingramcontent.com/pod-product-compliance
Lightning Source LLC
Chambersburg PA
CBHW031202020426
42333CB00013B/773